C000071106

1 MONTH OF
FREE
READING

at

www.ForgottenBooks.com

By purchasing this book you are eligible for one month membership to ForgottenBooks.com, giving you unlimited access to our entire collection of over 1,000,000 titles via our web site and mobile apps.

To claim your free month visit:

www.forgottenbooks.com/free947337

ISBN 978-0-260-42230-9
PIBN 10947337

ysical Item 43

THE ANNUAL PUBLICATION OF
THE SENIOR AND SOPHOMORE CLASSES
FOR THE STUDENTS OF THE
STATE TEACHERS COLLEGE
AT CLARION, PENNSYLVANIA

Nineteen Hundred and Thirty-Eight

P R E S E N

A T I O N

The Sequelle Staff has attempted in this, the 1938 Sequelle, to record faithfully the activities of 1938, its friendships, interests, and achievements. As you turn the leaves

T E D

Margaret A. Boyd, whose
ersonality has been an integral
ur years at Clarion State
College, we dedicate the
f 1938 in recognition of the
she has been, the friendship
freely proffered to everyone,
ntributions she has made to
.

CONTENTS · · ·

●

ADMINISTRATIO

Our President

Dr. Paul G. Chandler

To the Seniors

I wish to congratulate the senior class on your splendid work in helping to make the year's activities of the college a success. You have satisfactorily completed the last year of work, many of you with outstanding scholarship. Your influence has been felt on all student organizations and activities.

I shall follow with interest the course of each of you when you go out. In my mind you will always be students of Clarion, always welcome when you come back. Your teachers will be glad to see you and talk with you. Call on us at our homes and in our classrooms. Write to us occasionally. We will look forward with pleasure to your return at dances, homecomings, commencements, and reunions.

Come to these reunions, for each of you will always hold a place in the minds of your classmates peculiar to those who have gone through four years of undergraduate work together. Keep up your contacts. You can help each other in professional advancement. Visits with each other will be among your most enjoyable. Do not neglect them. Old friends are the best friends.

PAUL G. CHANDLER

Faculty

HELEN M. BARTON, M.A.
Physical Education
Columbia University

CHARLES F. BECKER, M.A.
Education
Columbia University

MARGARET A. BOYD, M.A.
English
University of Pittsburgh

CLAIR E. CAREY, M.A.
Mathematics
Harvard University

RENA M. CARLSON, M.A.
Librarian
University of Michigan

RALPH W. CORDIER, Ph.D.
Social Studies
Ohio State University

FRANCES EASLEY, M.A.
Primary Grades
George Peabody College

MILDRED GAMBLE, M.A.
Intermediate Grades
Columbia University

ANNA B. GRAHAM, B.S.
Junior High School Grades
Clarion State Teachers College

EFFIE BLANCHE HEPLER, B.S.
Primary Grades
Geneva College

GILBERT A. HOYT, M.S.
Junior High School Grades
Grove City College

CLARENCE A. KUHNER, M.S.
Geography
University of Wisconsin

BERTHA LEIFESTE, M.A.
Kindergarten-Primary Education
Columbia University

HARRY S. MANSON, M.A.
Science
Grove City College

ARIE E. MARWICK	VERA M. McKISSOCK	HELEN F. MOHNEY	BERTHA V. NAIR	FANNIE C. OWENS	DONALD D. PEIRCE	GLADYS RICH
AZEL M. SANDFORD	SARA SEYLER	HELEN D. SIMS	WALDO S. TIPPIN	HELEN WALTERS	LOTTIE WINGARD	

Faculty

MARIE MARWICK, M.A.
English
Columbia University

HAZEL SANDFORD, M.A.
Art
New York University

VERA M. McKISSOCK, M.A.
Intermediate Grades
University of Pittsburgh

SARA SEYLER
Dietitian
Worcester Domestic Science School

HELEN F. MOHNEY, B.S.
Intermediate Grades
University of Pittsburgh

HELEN D. SIMS, M.A.
Latin
University of Minnesota

BERTHA V. NAIR, M.A.
English
University of Pittsburgh

WALDO SAMUEL TIPPIN, M.A.
Physical Education
Columbia University

FANNIE CLAIRE OWENS, R. N.
Nurse
Oil City Hospital

HELEN WALTERS, B.A.
Primary Grades
Clarion State Teachers College

DONALD D. PEIRCE, Ph.D.
Science
University of Illinois

LOTTIE WINGARD
Registrar
Hoff Business College

GLADYS RICH, M.A.
Music
New York University

MARY C. DEVEREAUX
Librarian
University of Michigan

CLASSES

History of Senior Class

As we look back four years, we can see the class of 1938 as it was when it first entered C. S. T. C. We had fun trying to figure out our schedules. Six eight o'clocks—what a schedule!... Freshman week—carrying books in pillow cases. ... Impromptu chapel program... Costume day ... Mahatma Gandhi and others ... Mid-semester and first comments—studies do mean something here after all ... Miriam Marmein ... Smoky's interpretation ... Siberian Singers. ... Parents' weekend ... and last, but no means least—"*The Mikado*."

Sophomores ... What kind of freshies do we have to work on this year? ... Dedication of six new tennis courts .. The Boston Sinfonietts .. "*Anna Karenina*" ... "*A Tale of Two Cities*" ... Siberian Singers ... "*Let's Go Collegiate*" with Hitler, Stalin, Mussolini, and Hailie Selassie ... "*The Life of Louis Pasteur*." ... Farewells—farewells to those whose stay at Clarion terminates at the end of two short years.

Juniors ... The lily pond came into use ... What Juniors tossed what Sophomore into the pond? ... A new lily pond and fish pond came into being beside Seminary Hall ... The President's office was changed ... The library was enlarged. ... Miriam Marmein thrilled us again with her interpretive dancing ... College Players present "*The Show-Off*" ... Music and Art departments combine to produce "*H. M. S. Pinafore*" ... Siberian Singers ... Parents' weekend and "*Your Uncle Dudley*" ... Cook Forest picnic ... final exams.

Seniors ... on the last lap now ... Training School ... lesson plans ... we've dreaded this for four years ... supervising teachers are sympathetic enough to realize what causes that funny feeling in the stomach ... The Master Singers ... Miss Rich's operetta, "*The Lady Says Yes*" ... Mordan and Baer ... Ezra Rachlin ... Carola Gitana and Hero—Spanish dances this time ... College Players go Hungarian with "*Seven Sisters*"—a big hit ... Easter vacation ... Parents' weekend—the last one for us ... our college career draws to a close ... Graduation ... What does life hold in store for us? ... Farewell!

Joe Andreo

Joe's home is Darragh, Pennsylvania. A former high school coach suggested that he come to Clarion to play football. For four seasons Joe has juggled with center and half-back positions and has been a valuable man on the squad. He is president of Alpha Gamma Phi fraternity and a member of the Outdoor Club. Quiet, matter-of-fact, pleasant dispositioned—that's Joe—our "strong, silent man."

Michael Bedzyk

Mike first saw C. S. T. C. on registration day. He was lured to Clarion by a friend's promise of a job along with a college education. Now his ambition is to make Clarion a permanent home. Mike has won the titles of "C. S. T. C's best sport and athlete." He is a charter member and the first president of the Zeta Eta Phi fraternity. His majors are geography and social studies, and in addition he holds an elementary certificate.

David Bowser

Dave returned to C. S. T. C. this winter to complete his work for a bachelor of science degree in education. He first obtained a certificate in the elementary field in 1935 and has had two years teaching experience to his credit along with the acquisition of a wife and family. Dave is one of these silent wedded men who has little to say about himself.

1 9 3 8 • • • • SENIORS

[19]

Ruth Ehman

Ruth came back to C. S. T. C. the first semester of '37-'38 to finish and secure her bachelor's degree in educaton, specializing in the elementary field. She secured her two year certificate in 1932. She is a member of the Theta Alpha Lambda social sorority.

Ruth's pet hobby is dancing. She and Bailey were voted the best dance team on the campus in the popular "most and best ballot" this year.

Louise Furlong

Louise's interests are diversified. She has been a member of the Art, Press, Geography, International Relations, and Glee Clubs, Pi Gamma Mu honorary fraternity, and the College Players. Her apparent interest in clubs has won her the club editorship of the Sequelle for 1938. Louise's home is in Clarion. She is a member of the Delta Sigma Epsilon sorority and is the present secretary of that organization.

Florence Gathers

Daily for four years Flossie's "Chevey" has transported her from Shippenville to Clarion. It is so much a part of her that the thought of one leads to the other. Since sports are her hobby, naturally she devotes her extra-curricular time to such activities. She is a member of the Women's Athletic Association. For two successive years she has won the ping pong championship. She is a past president of the Sigma Delta Phi sorority.

SENIORS • • • • 1 9 3 8

Edward Jacobs

It was a case of "fisherman's luck" which brought Jake to C. S. T. C. His first visit to Clarion was the result of a fishing trip. Satisfied with a fair catch from the Clarion River, he decided to look around. He discovered the college. September found him enrolled. He is a member of Alpha Gamma Phi and Pi Gamma Mu fraternities, the Outdoor and Geography Clubs. He has also served on the Student Senate and the Men's Student Council.

Mary Joye Jones

Mary Joye, student composer, songster, one of C. S. T. C's typical students, president of the L. C. D's, hails from Strattanville, "on the East." She is a person whose name fits her to a "T". Her latest composition, "I'd Believe in You" has made a big hit on the campus. Throughout college she has played in all musical productions and has received a gold award for musical attainment. She receives a B.S. degree with majors in English and social studies.

Morgan Jones

Morgan has participated in practically every known activity on the campus. His famous characterization of prima donnas is among his many achievements. He is the present president of the Student Community Senate and has been a member of the following organizations: College Players, A Cappella Choir, Men's Glee Club, Male Quartet, and Phi Sigma Pi and Alpha Phi Alpha fraternities. Music is his hobby. Throughout his four years at C. S. T. C. he has been the school pianist.

1 9 3 8

SENIC

Dorothy Kaufman

Dot obtained her degree in secondary education at the end of the first semester of 1938. Geography and science are her majors. Her extra curricular activities have included the Geography Club, Press Club, Sequelle Staff, and International Relations Club. She is also a member of the Delta Sigma Epsilon sorority, of which she was treasurer for two years, and Pi Gamma Mu, national honorary fraternity in social studies.

Fred Marshall

"Freddie" is the "little man with big ideas" of the Senior Class. He has managed practically everything from basketball and football teams to the present personnel of the class. He is the president of the Alpha Phi Alpha fraternity, vice-president of the College Players, president of the Varsity C Club, and vice-president of the Student Senate. He is also a member of the Alpha Psi Omega, honorary fraternity.

William Marshall

Dividing his schooling between winter sessions at C. S. T. C. and summer sessions at Penn State, Bill has successfully obtained his bachelor of science degree in education in a period of three years. Bill is photography editor of the Sequelle for 1938. He is also a member of the Alpha Phi Alpha social fraternity besides belonging to the honorary fraternities, Phi Sigma Pi, Alpha Psi Omega, and Pi Gamma Mu. Bill was the students' choice of the fellow who would represent Clarion's most typical student.

SENIORS   •   1 9 3 8

Thomas Plyler

Tom has won his place at C. S. T. C. through his musical ability. His tenor voice has sung the leads in the *"Mikado"* and *"H. M. S. Pinafore."* He is a member of the Men's Quartet, the A Cappella Choir, Sequelle Staff, College Players, and Y. M. C. A. In addition to his membership in the Alpha Phi Alpha social fraternity, he is also a member of Phi Sigma Pi and Alpha Psi Omega honorary fraternities. He ranks first as C. S. T. C's best tennis player.

Edward Schierberl

"Swell" is Eddie's idea of C. S. T. C. in general. His interests include all the activities on the campus. He has played football for four years. However, his major sport interest lies in boxing. He has been a representative to the Student Senate for two years, a member of the Athletic Association, the Outdoor Club, Varsity C, and Geography Club. He is also a member of the Alpha Gamma Phi fraternity. One thing about Eddie which wins him a host of friends is his ever ready willingness "to do something."

Bronie Smolak

"Smokey" hails from Port Vue, Pennsylvania. He is another of C. S. T. C's best dancers in addition to being voted the best prospective teacher among the males of our campus. Specializing in mathematics and science "Smokey" obtains his B.S. in education, majoring in the secondary field. He is a member of the Alpha Gamma Phi fraternity and the Outdoor Club. He captained the basketball varsity through its 1938 season, playing both guard and forward positions.

Mae Stewart

Mae was graduated from Rimersburg High School in 1934. She has obtained her bachelor of science degree in education this spring, majoring in geography and social studies. She has been a member of the Hiking Club and the Geography Club, and is also a member of Pi Gamma Mu honorary fraternity. "My chief interest is map work," said Mae, when asked what she likes to do best. Her map work is one excellent proof of her scholastic ability in general.

Geraldine Thorne

Gerry has been one of the most versatile girls on the campus. She has served on the Student Community Senate for two years and has been a member of the following organizations: International Relations Club, Pi Gamma Mu, Pan-hellenic Council, Delta Sigma Epsilon sorority, Outdoor Club, Press Club, and the Women's Athletic Council. Her scholarship, popularity, and versatility have led her to her present editorship of the Sequelle.

Harry Wozniak

"Wozzie" is a graduate of Kittanning High School. Although his home is in Timblin, Pennsylvania, he has made Clarion an almost constant home for four years. During summer vacations he has worked at the glass factory. He has been janitor of the gymnasium, and for the past year he has been filling Teddy's shoes as part-time night watchman. He is a member of the Alpha Gamma Phi fraternity.

Laura Amsler

Thiel College certificated Laura in the secondary education field in mathematics. She came to C. S. T. C. this year as a post-graduate desirous of getting an additional certificate in the elementary field. Laura is a quiet, studious person. Her extra-curricular activities are the Y. W. C. A. and the N. A. C. E. organizations. Her home is in St. Petersburg, Pennsylvania.

Dora Boario

Leechburg has given us Dora. She first received her bachelor of science degree in the elementary field in 1937. Returning this year, she completed her work in the secondary field, adding to her teaching credentials majors in English and social studies. She is a member of the Delta Sigma Epsilon sorority, and Pi Gamma Mu, honorary fraternity. Other extra-curricular activities include College Players, A Cappella Choir, and N. A. C. E. Dora is also house president at Becht Hall.

1 9 3 8 • • POSTGRADUATES

JUNIORS • • • • •

HAROLD BAILEY—Here's your man, girls: brunette . . . loves to, and does it well, dance . . . provides conversational tidbits. History and science keep him busy (?)

VIRGIL BEARY— . . . gridiron football guard or tackle . . . huge in stature . . . funniest when serious. Major: elementary curriculum. May next fall see his return.

HAZEL BENNETT—With her changeable mood we find it rather hard to trace her train of thought. She's a kindergarten primary training teacher (!)

EARL BONNETT— . . . plucky athlete and scholar . . . remembered especially for anecdotal winter evenings in the upper dorm. Come back, boy, come back!

FERN BROOKS— . . . a "gal" of determination and level thought. Roman modes are known to her, for she is a Latin major.

JAMES CALL— . . . thespian and musician of the first water . . . plagued with pianoitis, saxaphobia, clarinetitis, and-oh well, that'll suffice. Majors: history and English.

ANNA MARY FOX—Even though her majors are science and history, she finds plenty of time for both warbling and one Jewell.

PAUL GRIFFIN—"Born with the gift of laughter, with the thought that the whole world's mad,"—and he? . . . history and English.

JOHN HASKELL—Married life, perhaps, makes this science and math major so serious; should more of us marry to obtain this virtue?

WALTER HASKELL—Would be outstanding in any journalistic enterprise; witness: late CALL editorship . . . attests full knowledge of women.

[26]

...BETH KANENGEISER—Although we find ...tty at times outspoken and opinionated, know her heart is always warm. Ele-...ntary division, her major.

ROLAND KIRKLAND—An historian and geog-rapher—well read—has wide experiences and enjoys relating them—a good sport—going places.

...ON KRIBBS—Industriousness has made ...d one of the most admirable fellows on campus. Gamut: from history-English ...basketball-football.

DEAN McKINNEY—Bound to be interested in anything: be it pithecanthropus erectus or Minsky's. Hopes to be an historian and a geographer.

...AN RENN—The College Players lay ...m to her, and with good reason! Should ...ome a splendid kindergarten instruct-...in due time.

BERNADINE STEWART—Scientist . . . geog-rapher . . . faithful . . . good-natured co-operative . . . ever-working, ever seeking something: happiest with found, desired reference.

...TON VOGEL—Pleasant . . . laughing . . . ...dsome . . . carefree . . . mathematician ...scientist . . . may he return with Earl ...is Alma Mater.

ARDELLE WHITMAN—Talkative . . full of action, and likes plenty of it, until: "yawn-time" (defined as end of every date!) Primary work intrigues her.

...WOLFF—As an artist she knows her ...s and colors. Joan may be small, but ...s always willing to do what she can ...you. Primary.

GRACE MOORE— . . . quiet . . . likeable: when there's something good in life, you always want (Ha!) "Moore" . . . insists she's no relation to THE Grace Moore.

•   •   •   •   •   **JUNIORS**

Graduating Sophomores

MARGARET AKERS	ELSIE BROWNSFIELD	ALTA COWAN		CATHERINE DAUGHERTY	WOODINE FREEDLINE	ESTHER HARTMAN
HELEN ALCORN	EILEEN BURKETT	OPAL DICKEY		CHARLOTTE DOVERSPIKE	PAUL GARMONG	GENEVA HEFFNER
MAURICE ANDERSON	LILLIAN COOK	MARY M. DONOHUE		LOUISE DUNKLE	GEORGEINE HAHN	ARTHUR HUMMEL

"Acres of diamonds". . . the stroller . . . imported from Indiana . . . good-hearted Elsie . . . the miniature athlete . . . "here comes Cookie" . . . the blonde nymph . . . all around sport . . . pep personified . . . "divinely fair and divinely tall" . . . me a senorita . . . life without a care . . . the athlete who made all varsities . . . clothes make the man . . . laughter holding both sides . . . tickler of the ivories . . . always hurrying . . . "talk little; listen much."

ELIZABETH JONES   JEAN LAUGHLIN   CATHERINE MINNS   ROBERT MOORE   EDITH PARK   FAY RUSSELL
ELLSWORTH KNARR   ELEANOR LAUGHNER   SAMUEL MONTANA   JENNIE MYERS   LOIS PFAFF   HELEN SAYERS

In secret . . . Michaelangelo . . . essence of poise . . . friendship's own daughter
. . . "Live to thyself" . . . noon librarian . . . Kirkland's better half . . . patience . . .
consistency . . . "laugh and the world laughs with you" . . . peanut lover . . .
chronic teaser . . . coquette . . . simplicity . . . immune from worries . . . "saving
up coupons" . . . silence is golden . . . all is well . . . C. S. T. C. heart-throb . . .
supremacy of males . . . little man . . . petite mademoiselles . . . child of Orpheus.

FAY SHERMAN   ETHELYN SMITH   RUSSEL SMITH   FRED SPENCE   STANLEY THOMPSON   MARTHA WASSUM
THELMA SMERKER   LAWRENCE SMITH   LUCILLE SNYDER   FRANK STEWART   HELEN WASSUM   HAZEL WEDEKIND

̶raduating Sophomores

̶ABERCROMBIE
    CHARLES BESKID
        CHESTER BYERLY
           LEROY CARLSON

̶EN DEILY
    LLOYD DIBB
        EDITH DINSMORE
           GRACE GILES

̶MER HORNER
    EVELYN JONES
        WILLIAM KISSEL
           PAUL LEHMAN

̶WAND LEWIS
    ALFRED MACDONALD
        JAMES MEYERS
           JOHN MOONEY

̶A MURDOCK
    BETTY MCCUE
        WILLIAM PHERO
           HELEN POPE

̶NFIELD PORT
    ZORA SAULA
        JOSEPH SCHIERBERL
           LUCILLE SEIGWORTH

̶BERT SHRIVER
    ARTHUR SMITH
        JANE SPEIDEL
           DONALD STROUPE

̶RRY TAYLOR
    MARSHALL TEETS
        EUGENE TRUNK
           PAUL TRUNK

Freshmen

First Row—Albert Andreo, Thomas Armagost, Phyllis Blum, Alene Botts, Margaret Bouquin, Anita Brown, Olga Burns, Russell Buzard, William Calderwood.

Second Row—William Elder, Carl Cheney, Louise Courson, Audrey Coyte, Edna May Eisenman, Robert Emerick, Louise Emhoff, Judd Fulton, Felix Galonski.

Third Row—Paul Giltinan, Pauline Hay, Louise Hess, Meade Hinderliter, James Imel, Robert Jewell, Jean Kapp, Dorothy Lehner, Ruth Lehner.

Fourth Row—Edythe Lucas, Jane MacMillan, Mary Marino, Hazel McCleery, Ronald McKinley, George McKissick, Anna Moyer, Leodra Mealy, Orville Myers.

Fifth Row—Edward Neuland, Eleanora Olson, Regina Phelan, Clair Reinsel, June Rhea, Eleanor Saul, Clair Rifenberrick, Allen Scheib, Jean Shaw.

Sixth Row—William Sheridan, Donald Shoup, Pauline Shumaker, Elizabeth Silvis, Deborah Singer, Ruth Slater, Kathleen Snyder, Stephen Snyder, Nanette Stahlman.

Seventh Row—Dorothy Stroupe, Lawrence Summerville, Mahlon Traister, Clara Trimble, Frances Whisner, Kathryn Whitehill, Theodore Williams, Merle Wiser, Clarence Yeany.

[31]

ORGANIZATIC

S

"Pleasures must not, nay cannot, be the business of a man of sense and character, but it may be, and is, his relief, his reward."

—Lord Chesterfield

Activities

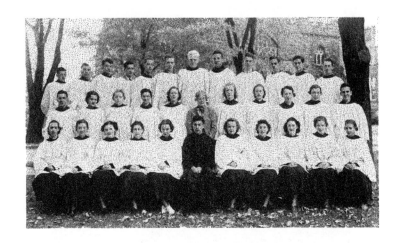

A Cappella Choir

The A Cappella Choir was enlarged this year to a membership of thirty-three voices.

It presented its first program on November 22, "*The Lady Says Yes,*" an operetta by Miss Gladys Rich. The men and maidens of Plymouth enacted the story of Miles Standish (James Call), Priscilla (Kathleen Snyder), and John Alden (Paul Giltinan). The supporting cast included: Prudence (Jane MacMillan,) Indian (Robert Jewell), comedian, Goodheart Manning (Rowland Lewis.)

The annual concert took place on February 10. This included Russian and American folksongs; selections by the orchestra; a violin solo by Bill Elder; a clarinet duet by Hazel Wedekind and James Call; and selections by the Men's Quartette consisting of Morgan Jones, Tom Plyler, Rowland Lewis, and James Call.

On February 22 the choir sang at the Presbyterian Church. On March 8 the choir, in new satin robes, took part in the Ground-Breaking program. The first choir trip was made to Ridgway on March 18.

A memorable event was the dinner dance on March 25, when awards were given to Mary Jones, Anna Mary Fox, Rowland Lewis, James Call, Hazel Wedekind, and Esther Hartman.

The Spring Concert was given on Parents' Day and included the cantata, "*The Triumph of Faith,*" by Miss Rich. It was also given in churches in Clarion and DuBois on May 1 and 15. Soloists were Anna Mary Fox and Tom Plyler.

Art Club

The Art Club is a group of students who are wide-awake to that which is beautiful and interesting from an artistic point of view. Most of the activities of the club have been devoted to handicrafts. Several new and unique projects were undertaken this year. Wood-burning was the most popular activity during the first semester. The boys were especially interested in the woodburning. Some of the other work undertaken by the club was the painting of wooden bowls, napkin rings, bracelets, brass craft, and Christmas cards.

The club was under the able supervision of Miss Sandford, who led the group in some interesting discussions, giving helpful hints which aided in perfecting the work.

On Tuesday, December 21, 1937, the club held a Beaux Arts Ball in the social room of Becht Hall. The group played games and danced, afterwards serving refreshments.

The officers for the first semester were: president, Ruth Ehman; vice-president, June Rhea; secretary-treasurer, Georgeine Hahn. The officers for the second semester were: president; Georgeine Hahn; vice-president, Charlotte Doverspike; secretary-treasurer, Eileen Burkett.

The motto of the organization may be told in the words of the poet Gulistan:

"If of thy mortal goods thou art bereft

And from thy slender store two loaves alone are left,

Sell one and, with the dole,

Buy hyacinths to feed thy soul."

The Association of Childhood Education

The Association of Childhood Education is a student branch of the National Association for Childhood Education. Any student training in the primary and intermediate fields, and any teacher or administrator interested in the work of this organization is eligible for membership.

The purposes of the club are: to gather and disseminate knowledge of the movement for the education of young children; to bring into active cooperation all childhood interests, including parent education to promote the progressive type of education in nursery schools, kindergartens, and primary grades; and to raise the standard of professional training for teachers and leaders in the field.

The club holds two types of meetings, educational and social. In the former, discussions are held on problems confronting teachers in their classrooms and community work with children. The annual program is presented by the Program Committee. The club held one meeting with the Kindergarten Mothers' Club, at which "Kindergarten as a Preparation for First Grade" was discussed. The group has enjoyed several social meetings: a Thanksgiving party, a Christmas party, and Washington's Birthday meeting.

There are thirty active members this year. The officers are: president, Dora Boario; vice-president, Ardelle Whitman; corresponding secretary, Hazel Bennett; recording secretary, Eleanor Laughner; treasurer, Opal Dickey; chairman of Childhood Education, Edith Park. Miss Bertha Leifeste is the club adviser.

The Community Senate

The Community Senate is the government body representing the students of the College. The Senate consists of twelve members. There are three representatives from the women day students, three from the resident women students, three from the men day students, and three from the resident men students.

Annual elections of representatives are held by each group represented, and from those elected, the entire student body elects the officers. The officers chosen for this year were: Morgan Jones, president; Fred Marshall, vice-president; and Geraldine Thorne, secretary.

From the Senate are selected various committees whose duties are to plan and regulate the affairs of the student body on the Clarion Campus. The social committee, which is headed by Eva Murdock, arranges the social calendar for the year. The chapel committee, composed of Dr. Peirce, Miss Sims, Miss Marwick, Geraldine Thorne, Fred Marshall, and Morgan Jones, plans and directs the lyceum numbers and the assembly programs. There are various other committees under the chairmanship of members of the Community Senate which function in the efficient management of the life of the students at Clarion.

The Senate plans and executes the program for the annual Parents' Week-end. During the first semester of every year the Senate co-operates with the administration by assisting the Freshmen in their orientation to their new surroundings.

The College Players

Club programs, varied and interes
were given by The College Playe
their regular bi-monthly meetings. U
the leadership of William Marshall
Dean McKinney, club presidents du
1937-1938, all activities have been
ducted in a manner that stimulated
interest in dramatics and insured
operation.

One-act plays presented in club n
ings included *"Red Carnations,"* "
pressed Desires," and *"The Soul
Professor,"* all directed and stage
members of the club. Two radio
gave the members who participat
little experience in microphone techn
A chapel play, *"A Wedding,"* was
joyed by the student body.

The most noteworthy productio
the year was the charming and spri
farce-comedy, *"Seven Sisters,"* ada
from the Hungarian original of F.
zég, by Edith Ellis. This three-act
was received with genuine appreci
by an audience of townspeople and
dents who were captivated by its
world flavor, colorful and striking
tumes, and effective staging. The
ers caught the spirit of gay abandon
that constitutes much of the char
the play. Miss Boyd gave inval
aid in make-up. Stage setting and
tumes were designed by Miss Mar
who also directed the play.

The College Players enjoyed
social affairs during the year. Per
the most unique of these was the G
Trek and Encampment in May. D
song, and secret Romany rites are
the camp fire made this occasion o
be remembered by the Players.

Geography Club

The officers elected for the Geography Club during the school year of 1937-1938 were as follows: co-presidents Dorothy Kaufman, Harry Wozniak; vice-president, Bernadine Stewart; secretary-treasurer, Marian Renn.

The outline of the year's work centered around the collection of free materials available to teachers in the field.   Several compiled lists were divided among the club members, who, in turn, sent for material which proved to be of educational value or of interest.   The final exhibit held real value for those interested in increasing their supply of teaching material.

Several trips were taken by the club to places which would prove of interest to students as prospective teachers.   The first trip included a tour of Oil City's foundry, refining plant, and bakery.   This was a half day trip.

Another trip included a visit at the local glass plant, a worth-while subject for a field trip, especially to teachers who will be employed in this vicinity.   A trip was also made to a near-by coal mine.

Other activities of the club for this year were: showing of geographical moving pictures, talks by our sponsor, Mr Kuhner, and other members, and parties which were held in the gym.

Hostess Club

The Hostess Club opened the 1937-38 term with the subject of serving. First the girls studied "teas," both formal and informal, later holding a tea in Becht Hall. Then they studied the serving of luncheons and dinners.

The Hostesses then turned to the subject of "Care of the Skin and the Use of Make-up." Much time was also spent on the subject of the care of the hair and the matter of suitable coiffures. The girls were eager to solve the problem of how to dress on a college girl's allowance.

Next the Hostesses turned their practical eyes toward decorations and flower arrangements. They examined the girls' rooms in Becht Hall to see for themselves what was good and bad in the way of interior decorations.

The Hostesses turned to polite society and to "courtesy" for their next subjects. They thought it practical to learn the "do's" and "dont's" concerning introductions, receptions, and week-end parties.

They served the tea for the Ground-breaking reception. Their help was also indispensable at the Parents' Day tea. The Club bought several games for Becht Hall. In spite of all this work the Hostess Club girls found time and energy for a little "fun." They finished the first semester with a candy party at Mrs. Hoyt's and closed this term with a dinner party.

Outdoor Club

The purpose of the Outdoor Club, as its name indicates, is gaining a better appreciation of the out-of-doors; and the activities of the club center around the good fellowship which may be found in the open.

The club consists of twenty-four members. New members are elected in the fall of each school term by the unanimous vote of the old members. The club, one of the most active on the campus, usually has a lengthy waiting list. A picnic supper in Wilson's Woods was held for the initiates this year.

A number of group outings have taken place in Cook Forest during the year. The main event in October was a steak-fry and hike. The group activities for November included a hike, followed by a lunch; and a six-o'clock breakfast in one of the club's favorite haunts, Wilson's Woods. During the winter months, when conditions were suitable, the members went tobogganing and ice-skating.

The membership consists of twelve women and twelve men, and the club sponsor is Mr. Harry Manson.

The activities for the spring were numerous, including: a tramp to the Indian Cave, hikes along the trails of wooded sections in the vicinity of Clarion, bicycling at the Fairgrounds, and several roller skating parties. In the latter part of May the club enjoyed a moonlight hike.

Press Club

The Press Club was organized a number of years ago by students interested in journalism. Since that time the organization has enlarged its activities until now it is one of the leading organizations on the campus.

"The 'Clarion Call,' the printed voice of Clarion State Teachers College," is published monthly. All college news and publicity appearing in non-campus papers is written by a staff member. The Press Club has cooperated with the College in sending out press notices to the various papers in the service area. Students active in College life thus receive recognition in their home town papers. The "Clarion Call" has a large exchange list and is circulated throughout the State. At the present time the "Call" is leading an alumni drive to gather funds with which to purchase a college bus.

The Press Club has received an invitation to form a chapter of Alpha Phi Gamma. Alpha Phi Gamma is the only honorary, nation-wide, co-educational, journalistic fraternity in existence.

The annual club trip was made to Pittsburgh in April. Here the new Post-Gazette building, Cathedral of Learning, Carnegie Tech, Connelley Trade School, with dinner and show following were the center of interest. The Club banquet held April 12, was the outstanding social function of the Club.

The officers of the Club for the year 1937-38 were: editor, Walter Haskell, Jr.; secretary, Lucille Seigworth; faculty adviser, Miss Nair.

Sequelle Staff

In the spring of 1937 the members of the Senior Class elected Geraldine Thorne editor and Bronie Smolak business manager of the 1937-38 annual publication, "The Sequelle." The remainder of the staff was selected by the editor at the beginning of the school year from the members of the Senior and Sophomore classes.

The members of the staff are: Geraldine Thorne, editor; Bronie Smolak, business manager; Betty McCue, Greeks; Louise Furlong, organizations; William Marshall, photography; Catherine Daugherty and Eileen Burkett, art; Chester Byerly, feature; Fay Russell and Lucille Seigworth, typists; Eva Murdock, women's athletics; Fred Marshall, men's athletics; Tom Plyler, literary editor.

Work on the publication began in the fall of 1937. The contract for the photography was let to the Zamsky Studios, Philadelphia, Pennsylvania. New angle shots of the campus and buildings, group pictures, and individual photographs of every faculty member and student were taken.

Write-ups of the various organizations and activities were arranged and assembled under the supervision of Miss Nair, the "Sequelle" adviser. Professor Clarence Kuhner acted as business adviser.

The Jahn-Ollier Engraving Company, Chicago, Illinois, was in charge of the engraving, and the Gray Printing Company, DuBois, Pennsylvania, did the printing.

The members of the Staff wish to express their most sincere appreciation to those who cooperated in numerous ways in the publication of the Sequelle.

Women's Student Council

The Women's Student Council is the governing body of Becht Hall, the girls' dormitory. The purpose of this organization is to deal with and control such matters of student life as are entrusted to the organization; to foster among the women students greater individual responsibility; to see that a high standard of life and culture is maintained; and to develop a spirit of cooperation between the parents and the president and faculty of the College.

The duties of the Women's Student Council are: to enforce all rules and regulations; to deal with cases of discipline; to make all necessary rules to secure the best conduct in student life; and to promote a home-like atmosphere in considering the personal problems of each individual, in purchasing publications for the lounge, in sending floral tributes, and in extending condolences in times of illness or death.

This group is composed of nine members under the supervision of the dean of women, Miss Sims, who is at all times the adviser and counselor of the organization.

The officers of the Council for this year were: Eleanor Laughner, president; Grace Giles, vice-president; Margaret Akers, secretary-treasurer. Dora Boario was president of the entire house during the year. The other members were: Margaret Akers, Eleanor Laughner, Katherine Minns, Dora Boario, Helen Deily, Grace Giles, Jean Shaw, Audrey Coyte, and Eleanor Saul.

Young Men's Christian Association

The Young Men's Christian Association has a direct interest in the spiritual, moral, and physical life of our young men. Through its meetings it is constantly endeavoring to further a spirit of understanding and to foster a feeling of tolerance and fellowship.

The attendance of the 'Y'', although never large, has been encouragingly constant throughout the year. Those who have filled the executive and administrative officers are: Robert Moore, president; Robert Jewell, vice-president; Harry Wozniak, secretary-treasurer. The efforts of these officers have been efficiently supplemented by the splendid cooperation of all members.

The ten or twelve members who attend regularly have been many times repaid for their efforts by being privileged to hear interesting talks given by Dr. Chandler, Mr. Carey, Mr. Becker, Dr. Peirce, and Mr. Kuhner. These individuals, representing the executive staff of the college, are well qualified to speak before the group. Another form of activity enjoyed by the members is the informal discussions of vital problems that the Young Men's Christian Association might be able to help solve. Social meetings in the gymnasium are also a part of the program.

The "Y" provides a splendid example of the small organization at its best. In attaining its ends, the "Y" is proud to attribute much of its success to the guidance and help of Mr. Charles Becker; the organization's efficient adviser.

Young Women's Christian Association

The Young Women's Christian Association tries to meet the spiritual needs of all the girls on the campus. It aims to create a spirit of sisterhood and to promote friendship among the girls. It is most influential in fostering the development of a personal philosophy of conduct and morality in the individual member.

A devotional service is conducted each Wednesday evening from seven to eight o'clock. A leader, chosen by the cabinet, conducts the meeting and the members contribute their ideas. Special effort is made to build up those characteristics necessary to a successful teacher. Miss Sims, the group adviser, helps to discuss difficult problems, and her suggestions are most valuable. Special music, prayers, and poems add interest.

During the school year, the "Y" has enjoyed a variety of activities. The "Big Sister" movement at the freshmen reception and a pajama party on the first night of school assisted the freshman girls in making their acquaintances. The program for Parents' Week-end was a success. An outdoor party was planned for May, and a local minister engaged as a speaker.

The officers of the "Y" Cabinet are: president, Helen Deily; secretary, Eleanor Laughner; treasurer, Ethelyn Smith. It is felt that every girl should be interested in the Christian life and do all she can to make the Young Women's Christian Association a success.

Autographs

"The isles of Greece, the isles of Greece!
Where burning Sappho loved and sung.
Where grew the arts of war and peace,-
Where Delos rose, and Phoebus sprung!
Eternal summer gilds them yet,
But all, except their sun, is set."

—Byron "Don Juan"

Greek

Societies

Alpha Upsilon Cast

The Alpha Upsilon Cast of the national honorary dramatic fraternity, Alpha Psi Omega, is pleased to report that its members have experienced the most progressive season in its history. Four eligible neophytes were initiated late in October at a Cast banquet. They were Earl Bonnett, Morgan Jones, Fred Marshall, and Tom Plyler.

Early in November, the Cast motored to Pittsburgh to see the play, KING RICHARD II, at a Nixon Theatre matinee, in which Maurice Evans starred. This was followed by dinner, before the group left the city.

Last February, while attending a tea served by Miss Margaret Boyd, Cast adviser, they made final arrangements to attend BURY THE DEAD by Irwin Shaw. This play was splendidly produced in the Allegheny Playshop at Allegheny.

Cast-director William Marshall reports that the organization has been active in leadership of dramatic enterprises on the campus. Various members have served as student-directors of THE COLLEGE PLAYERS' chapel and club plays and skits. Cooperation and faithfulness of all the members has been evident on many occasions, especially in aiding in the production of the major drama of the year, SEVEN SISTERS by Edith Ellis, in April.

They look forward to the new season, during which it is hoped that the alumni of the Alpha Upsilon Cast may aid in producing a play, strictly limited to the members.

The national, honorary, educational fraternity, Phi Sigma Pi, is a fraternity whose membership is devoted to students with a professional educational interest. This year's activity program included several social gatherings, business and professional meetings, and initiations of new members.

The officers of the school year 1937-38 were : Thomas M. Plyler, president; Paul Griffin, vice-president; James Call, secretary; William Marshall, corresponding secretary; and Walter Haskell, treasurer.

There were two initiations. The first initiation was held in Music Hall on November 5, 1937. The second was held at Dr. Peirce's house on December 17, 1937. At the first initiation, Dr. Cordier, Benton Kribbs, Robert Shriver, Paul Lehman, and Chester Byerly were admitted as members. At the second initiation, Fred Marshall was admitted. Following the initiation, refreshments were served and some interesting phases of education were discussed.

Because of the small student body and increased extra-curricular load upon each member, it was regarded inadvisable to construct a project as in past years.

One worthwhile trip the fraternity took this spring was to the Allegheny Observatory of Astronomy at Pittsburgh. A two hour lecture, examination and manipulation of the telescopes, proved very interesting and educational. The same evening, the men also went to the theatre. The annual banquet on April 27 was a great success. The men invited their women friends to the dinner dance, and everybody had an unusually pleasant evening.

Pi Gamma Mu

Pi Gamma Mu is a social studies honor society limited to juniors, seniors, graduate students, alumni, and instructors. It aims to instill into the mind of the individual a scientific attitude toward all social questions.

For several years Pennsylvania Iota at Clarion has organized and guided the International Relations Club for students not necessarily belonging to Pi Gamma Mu but, nevertheless, interested in international affairs. This club has access to the books and pamphlets issued by the Carnegie Endowment for International Peace and is organized into groups for the discussion of current world problems. Such topics as British Foreign Policy and the Empire, Conflicts and Cooperation across the Pacific, Europe and International Security, and the Western Hemisphere have been discussed and analyzed in view of recent events of world importance.

Pi Gamma Mu proper is led by Edward Jacobs, president; William Marshall, vice-president; Dora Boario, secretary-treasurer; and Paul Griffin, sergeant-at-arms. These officers also take charge at the bi-monthly meetings of International Relations Club. The society receives "Social Science" published quarterly as an open forum.

Last fall Pi Gamma Mu brought to the College Samuel B. Wyer, who gave the students much food for thought in his various discussions on civilization. The future will probably bring other contributions by way of the speaker's platform which will give an insight into many social questions.

The Pan-hellenic Council

The Pan-hellenic Council is the governmental body representing the five sororities, Sigma Sigma Sigma, Delta Sigma Epsilon, Lambda Chi Delta, Sigma Delta Phi, and Theta Alpha Lambda.   There is one active and one silent member from each of these sororities.   After Miss Boyd's resignation as guide and faculty adviser last year, the girls chose Miss Helen Sims for the coming years.

The officers for the first semester were: president, Helen Alcorn, Theta Alpha Lambda; secretary-treasurer, Hazel Wedekind, Sigma Sigma Sigma; for the second semester: president, Geraldine Thorne, Delta Sigma Epsilon; secretary Georgeine Hahn, Lambda Chi Delta; treasurer, Bernadine Stewart, Sigma Delta Phi.

This year the Council gave its second scholarship fund equal to one semester's tuition. This is given each year to an upper-class girl who is chosen by two Pan-hellenic representatives, Miss Helen Sims, and Dr. Paul Chandler.

The first social function of the year was a tea, which was held on September 22. All the women students on the campus were invited, and the old and new became acquainted.

The annual Pan-hellenic dinner was held on December 17. Everything was carried out for a gala Christmas party with a short play entitled "Mistletoe" to furnish entertainment. On April 8 the Pan-hellenic balloon dance was held. To this dance were invited sorority women living in the community who were affiliated with any national sorority, also the sponsors and patronesses.

Delta Sigma Epsilon Sorority

During the past year, Alpha Zeta chapter of Delta Sigma Epsilon, a national educational sorority, has met with much success. The success is attributed to the cooperation of the actives, pledges, alumnae, patronesses, and her able sponsor, Miss Barton.

Her activities of the year can be classed in three groups: namely, social functions, social service acts, and study of society and sorority problems and ethics; also included was an official inspection by Mrs. Nye, national treasurer of Delta Sigma Epsilon.

The first social function of importance was the fall "rush" party, which proved to be significant, for eight girls were pledged.

The biggest social function of the year was the meeting of the First Province, held at Clarion on April 2 and 3. This conference was well attended, and boosted Alpha Zeta Chapter immensely, since it was the first meeting of its kind in the history of the organization.

The social service acts included a contribution toward purchasing a gift basket for a needy family at Thanksgiving; a Christmas party given by the members for the kindergarten children; and the furnishing of entertainment at a Christmas party, sponsored by the Clarion Woman's Club.

The officers for the past year were: Geraldine Thorne, president; Eleanor Laughner, vice-president; Dora Boario, corresponding secretary; Louise Furlong, recording secretary; and Dorothy Kaufman and Grace Giles, co-treasurers.

The officers elected for the year 1937-38 were: president, Mary Jones; vice-president, Zora Saula; secretary, Ardelle Whitman; treasurer, Marian Renn.

During the first few weeks of school, the chief interest of the Lambda Chi's was equipping and decorating the new sorority room. They were successful to such a degree that they have spent much of their free time there during the year. The rushing efforts with a dinner at the Coffee Shop were well rewarded by bringing eight new members into the sorority.

The sorority girls still feature in all activities on the campus: they have six members in the College Players, six in A Cappella Choir, four in the Geography club, and five in the Outdoor club.

The sorority newspaper is still a tradition, this year being under the editorship of "Manny" Renn. The loan fund also still stands and has increased for the use of Lambda Chi girls.

The year's activities have taken the form of hikes, weiner roasts, informal parties at members' homes, and a mid-semester slumber party. Cookie sales, yarn dolls, candy sales, and individual identification stickers added money to the treasury. Plans for the annual camping trip at Lake Erie loom larger than ever this year, and the members look forward to it with much anticipation.

Sigma Delta Phi

The Sigma Delta Phi sorority started the events of the year with one of those traditional picnics in Wilson's Woods. The first semester rush party held in the Eastern Star rooms, the pledge party, and initiation were three of the biggest events of the year. For the second semester rush party an evening of fun was spent at the home of Miss Bernadine Stewart. The members also have happy memories of a dinner given last fall at the home of an alumna, Mrs. Ruth Cambell Hood of Franklin, Pennsylvania. Another delightful occasion was the Christmas party held at Miss Nair's home. The sorority girls spread a bit of cheer at Christmas by packing a Christmas basket for an unfortunate family. The girls also bought gifts for a number of children.

The sorority girls were gratified to be assigned this year a sorority room in Becht Hall. Much enthusiasm, effort, and time were spent decorating and furnishing the room.

The sorority sponsor is Miss Bertha V. Nair. The officers for the year were: Eva Murdock, president; Charlotte Doverspike, vice-president; Fay Sherman, treasurer; and Eileen Burkett, secretary. Panhellenic representatives are: Bernadine Stewart, active; Eva Murdock, silent. The patronesses of the sorority are: Mrs. Harry Wilson, Mrs Lloyd Weaver, Mrs. James Hess, Mrs. Milo Smathers, all of Clarion; and Mrs. Anabel Ralston of Butler, Pennsylvania.

Sigma Sigma Sigma

Sigma Sigma Sigma is a national educational sorority. It holds the honor of being the first educational sorority organized.

The first rush party in the fall was a dinner held at Cook Forest in a log cabin. The girls spent the evening before an open fireplace, playing games, roasting marshmallows and dancing. As a result of rush week, they pledged three girls: Deborah Singer, Ruth Lehner, and Helen Hollar. Deborah Singer entertained the group with a tobogganing party one cold wintry evening. For the second semester rush week a party was held in Becht Hall in the social room. The evening was spent in dancing. The patronesses, Mrs. Kuhner, Mrs. Riley, Mrs. Long, and Mrs. Fitzgerald, entertained the sorority at the home of Mrs. Kuhner.

The members were all gratified by a visit in September by Mrs. Morrison, a national officer, who gave them much help and inspiration.

As Sigma Sigma Sigma looks forward to the future, the members hope that the new year will mean a continuance of the friendship and enjoyable activities of the past one.

Tri Sigma carries out a social service plan. This year they gave food and clothing to poor families and gave scrap books to hospitals.

The officers are: president, Esther Hartman; vice-president, Hazel Wedekind; secretary, Alta Cowan; and treasurer, Mary Donahue. Tri Sigma is under the able sponsorship of Miss Mildred Gamble.

Theta Alpha Lambda

The girls of the Theta Alpha Lambda sorority busied themselves early this fall with preparations for their annual rush party. The party this year was a dinner party held at the Coffee Shop in Clarion. At this party they discovered that they had a palmist in their midst, and she has been kept quite busy since telling the girls their future.

After initiations were over, the Theta's decided to get better acquainted with each other, and so devised a program wherein each member introduced another, telling about her hobbies, family, school life, and ambitions. These introductions proved very interesting and helpful in acquainting the new girls with the old.

After the beginning of the second semester and the change of officers the girls again settled down to steady work in the sorority. Much was added to the meetings by a series of programs, conducted by the girls about their hobbies. These programs proved entertaining and educational. The girls, naturally enthusiastic about their work, gave animated talks and demonstrations.

All during the year the girls grouped together for various activities, such as hiking before breakfast, meeting at Sweetland for a "coke", and just getting together for heart to heart talks. There is a fine feeling of fellowship among the girls, and the Thetas gain much by their intimate associations with one another.

Alpha Gamma Phi

The social fraternity of Alpha Gamma Phi opened its 1937-1938 school year with the following capable officers: Bronie Smolak, president; Joe Andreo, vice-president; Alfred MacDonald, secretary; and Joseph Schierberl, treasurer. Thirteen men were left from last year to carry on the work.

The first problem that confronted the fraternity was the selection of the rushees, who perhaps would become future members, to take the place of the graduated members. A rush party was held in the gymnasium in September, with the freshmen fellows as the honor guests. Eleven of these freshmen joined the fraternity.

The social activities of the first semester consisted of a masquerade party which was held at Camp Coffman on November 1, a roller skating party, as guests of Alpha Phi Alpha fraternity; and a Christmas party at the home of Paul Trunk.

The officers of the fraternity for the second semester were: Joe Andreo, president; Harry Wozniak, vice-president; John Sershen, historian; Paul Trunk, secretary; and Paul Griffin, treasurer. Two new members, Gene Campbell and Kenneth Rodgers, were taken into the fraternity on February 21.

The most outstanding social event of the year was the inter-fraternity dance on March 12, with Barry Blue and his orchestra furnishing the music. The climax of all social activities was the fraternity banquet, held near the close of the school year.

Alpha Phi Alpha

Alpha Phi Alpha started the 1937-38 season with the annual fall outing at Camp Coffman. At this time Rifenberrick, Snyder, Buzard, McKinley, Neuland, Kirkland, Armagost, Sheridan, McKissick, Vogel, and Meyers were informally inducted into the brotherhood. Formal initiation followed a week later.

November eighth was the date of a party held in the chapel gymnasium. Volleyball and basketball were the order of the evening, and doughnuts and cider provided the refreshments.

Paul Lehman played host for the annual Christmas party. Games were played until refreshments were served. Afterwards some very appropriate gifts were distributed.

The next event on the social calendar was the spaghetti supper held in Mr. Manson's room. After a short business meeting the rest of the evening was spent playing cards.

Jewell and Elder furnished the entertainment for our next gathering, when they received their informal initiation. On the following Monday the formal initiation was held.

The high spot of the year, however, was reached with the inter-fraternity dance. Barry Blue and his orchestra furnished the music for what was admittedly the best fraternity dance ever held on this campus.

The advent of a new fraternity on the campus necessitated the formation of an inter-fraternity council. The representatives were Fred Marshall, Morgan Jones, and Tom Plyler.

The officers for the past year were: president, Fred Marshall; vice-president, Bill Marshall; corresponding secretary, Morgan Jones; and treasurer, Robert Shriver.

Zeta Eta Phi

The Zeta Eta Phi Fraternity, being newly organized, has spent the greater part of the year perfecting its organization. However, the task has not hindered the members from being very active in all other fields.

In spite of possessing the newest name on the campus, they were able to pledge twelve members in the current school year. They are, however, rapidly building up their prestige.

No member will readily forget the informal initiation. Having in mind the purpose of making the candidates as ridiculous as possible, the fraternity held the initiation in the Garby Theater, where some seven hundred people laughed at the miseries of the pledges. This proved highly successful and sufficiently embarrassing to make it an annual occurrence.

The social functions within the fraternity have been too numerous to mention. Some parties were held in conjunction with meetings, and many others in which skiing, hiking, skating and moving pictures claimed the interest. Christmas provided an opportunity for holding a Holiday Raffle. This little venture gained three lucky students valuable prizes. Members of the organization played an important part in arranging the highly successful inter-fraternity dance.

The regular meetings provided time for discussion of important problems of the day. Officers are: Mike Bedzyk, president; Jim Meyers, vice-president; and Lawrence Smith, secretary-treasurer.

ATHLE

HELEN M. BARTON

The department of physical education for women endeavors to fulfill a triple assignment and to give each division its relative attention. Many girls come to us with a limited acquaintance with the sport's field, and first of all we must broaden their scope and afford them greater opportunity for appreciation of physical activity. Recreational values are stressed in this procedure, and each girl is urged to find some form of sport in which she may satisfy her individual tastes, that after graduation enjoyment may continue in this field.

Although we pay attention to recreation and student health, we must not neglect the fact that this is a teacher training institution and that we have a decided responsibility in this regard. While we do not specialize in this field, our students have been able because of their work here to fill positions which demand a coaching knowledge of sports and teaching ability in rhythmic activities of the elementary schools.

The furtherance of individual adjustment to the social group is the least discernible of the department's program, but perhaps that of most vital importance to the individual's success. The gymnasium and playfield are the laboratories in which this study in smoother human relationships is carried forward.

Women's Athletic Council

The Women's Athletic Council aims to develop an interest in athletics, and to foster clean living, high standards of sportsmanship, and purposeful service in campus activities.

Each year the council plans an intra-mural sports program of various tournaments between the freshmen and sophomore girls. These tournaments are coached by W. A. C. members. The girls elect their own captains and managers, and these in turn select a class team from their squad. The major sports include: hockey, soccer, basketball, volley ball, and softball. Horseshoe pitching was added this year. From the two class teams an honorary varsity is chosen. Eligibility for the varsity is determined by these factors: attendance at practices, playing ability, and good sportsmanship. At the close of the year the ten girls having the highest number of points receive varsity letters and automatically become members of the Women's Athletic Council. Old members of the council are awarded letters with stars according to the number of years of service, if they participate in two sports and coach one, or coach two and participate in one.

This year the W. A. C. sponsored a tournament of such minor sports as ping-pong, shuffle-board, and badminton. At the Ground-breaking ceremony the girls presented an excellent exhibition of various sports.

The officers for W. A. C. this year were: Geraldine Thorne, president; Eileen Burkett, vice-president; and Helen Deily, secretary. The other members were: Georgeine Hahn, Lillian Cook, Florence Gathers, and Eva Murdock.

Hockey

The women's intramural athletic program opened with a hockey tournament. The sophomores with more experience and training won the first two games which were played, thus copping the first contest. The score of the first game was 5-0; the second game ended with a score of 5-1.

The weather for hockey was ideal. Both freshmen and sophomores played persistently in both games, after which there was a display of stoved fingers and bruised shins. The freshmen were coached by Eva Murdock with Audrey Coyte as captain and Peggy Bouquin as manager. Georgeine Hahn was coach of the sophomores; Woodine Freedline was captain and Eileen Burkett was manager.

The hockey varsity, which was chosen by the Women's Athletic Council, consisted of the following women: Anita Brown, Audrey Coyte, Peg Donahue, Charlotte Doverspike, Woodine Freedline, Joan Kroh, Edythe Lucas, Jennie Myers, Deborah Singer, Clara Trimble, and Hazel Wedekind.

Soccer was the second sport scheduled for the fall season. Eva Murdock and Georgeine Hahn were again the coaches selected for this sport, but the weather interfered and prevented the completion of the tournament. Several attempts were made, but the rain persisted in coming on the days on which the soccer games were planned. However, the girls who reported for practice were awarded fifty points toward a letter.

Basketball

The basketball tournament was probably the most exciting contest of the year. There was a vivid and fiery rivalry between the freshman and sophomore teams which resulted from the teams being well matched. The first game ended with the freshmen, coached by Gerry Thorne, defeating the sophomores, coached by Lillian Cook, with a score of 21-18. Then came the second game during which the sophomores showed much better team work, but again they were defeated; the score was 33-17. The last game was also won by the freshmen, but only after a hard fought battle. The score was tied throughout practically the whole game, until the last few minutes when the freshmen forged ahead leaving the score 22-21.

The girls who were chosen for the varsity team are: Evelyn Jones, Betty Kanengeiser, Jane MacMillan, Anita Brown, Peggie Bouquin, and Woodine Freedline.

Volley Ball

The volley ball tournament, unlike basketball, was strictly in the sophomores favor. This was to be expected since the sophomores had been trained last year. However, the freshmen put up a hard fight for each game they lost. The sophomores were captained by Gerry Thorne, managed by Jane Speidel, and coached by Florence Gathers. The freshmen has as their officials the following: captain, Peggy Bouquin; manager, Anita Brown; Coach, Eileen Burkett.

The volley ball varsity consisted of: Woodine Freedline, Jane Speidel, Jennie Myers, Charlotte Doverspike, Clara Trimble, Eleanora Olson, Evelyn Jones, and Anita Brown.

Letter Winners of 1938

CHARLOTTE DOVERSPIKE was one of the few sophomores who participated in all sports. Her favoirte games were hockey and basketball. She was chosen for the volley ball varsity

PEGGY BOUQUIN teamed with Anita Brown in managing most of the freshman teams. These girls were also coupled in the center section of the basketball. Peggy made the basketball varsity.

REGINA PHELAN was interested in both major and minor sports. She first made herself known on the hockey field, where she revealed great determination.

EVELYN JONES made a place for herself when she was chosen to take Fay Russell's place on the basketball team. She was an excellent guard.

JENNIE MYERS was a conscientious athlete who refused to give up. She was a good sport, and willingly cooperated in all the tournaments.

CLARA TRIMBLE was that dynamic freshman, whose skill in intramurals caused the sophomores no little discomfort. She had a wicked serve in volley ball.

ELEANORA OLSON was one of those sports-minded freshmen who attended practices regularly. She deserves commendation on her good sportsmanship and volley ball playing.

Letter Winners of 1938

WOODINE FREEDLINE, the sophomore star player, made all the varsity teams. One of her outstanding feats was making twenty-two successive points in a volley ball game.

JANE MACMILLAN was the freshmen's outstanding forward on the basketball team. Her long shots fairly took one's breath away. She was also a good hockey player.

PEG DONAHUE, was the speedy little sophomore player, who always got the ball from the opponent. She did her best work in hockey.

EDYTHE LUCAS, another freshman who starred in hockey, put fear into the hearts of her opponents by her hard-fighting facial expressions.

ANITA BROWN could always be depended on. She was frequently chosen as one of the freshmen's officials. She played a good game of basketball.

HAZEL WEDEKIND was manager of the sophomore hockey, soccer, and basketball teams. She was teamed with Lillian Cook in the minor sports tournament. They won the badminton contest.

Men's Athletics

WALDO S. TIPPIN

As usual the first activity in the department of physical education for men was inter-collegiate football. The team had a great many new men, and it took some time for them to adjust themselves to a system of football somewhat new to them. However, at the close of the season the team was functioning well and finished with a record of three games won and three lost. Marked improvement was seen this season in sharp blocking and tackling. Perhaps the most glaring weakness was the inability to convert the point after a touchdown, which cost two games.

Basketball got under way about the middle of December. Here again there were many new men, and various combinations were tried. Several games were lost by close scores, and then the team began to click, winning the last four games of the year.

The spring schedule consisted of eight baseball games and ten tennis matches. Baseball was revived after a lapse of several years. Tennis entered upon its third year as an intercollegiate activity, and this year the Athletic Council voted to recognize it as an inter-collegiate sport and hence award the Varsity "C" for a degree of proficiency in it.

The major sports program was interspersed with intramural sports of touch football, basketball, and volleyball.

Varsity "C" Club

The Varsity "C" Club is an organization on the Campus for men who have earned their letters by participating in one of the major sports.

The requirements for winning the awards are set up each year by the Men's Athletic Council. Letters are given to the men meeting these standards by the cooperative association, while additional awards of sweaters are given by the club.

Until the last three years it was the custom for each man to buy his own sweater, but since that time the club has been able to pay for these awards out of its treasury. In order to do this, it has been found necessary to put on several money-making campaigns each year.

This year the club sponsored a turkey raffle at Thanksgiving, the annual Alumni basketball game, and a refreshment stand at the Ground-breaking dance. These affairs along with the life membership dues paid by each member netted enough for the club to meet its expenses. Plans were made for the club to sponsor a movie before the close of the year. The club has also enjoyed several social functions.

Cooperativeness, sportmanship, and fair play are the ideals stressed by the organization, and all of the members strive to live up to those ideals.—The officers for this year were: president, Fred Marshall; and secretary-treasurer, Charles Beskid.

Tennis

Tennis as an inter-collegiate sport is not new at Clarion. In fact, during the early '20's, Clarion maintained a tennis team with an enviable record. At that time, there was, annually, an Inter-Normal Tournament between Indiana, California, and Clarion. The popularity of the game may be evidenced by an excerpt, "Upon reaching California, the (Clarion) team was greeted by the entire school." Another," ... glad and proud of the noble champions of our school ... celebrated by a parade around town."

Then, for a period of years (1925-1935), this delightful and wholesome outdoor sport, older, yes, decades older than other prevalent inter-collegiate sports at Clarion, suffered a lapse. But the revival of inter-collegiate tennis for Clarion occurred in the spring of 1936 when special impetus was given by our newly-constructed, hard-surfaced. courts, That year we met Grove City, Indiana, Slippery Rock, and the Clarion Tennis Club.

Our inexperience and lack of adequate training have affected our degree of success these past two seasons; however, the second season (1937) showed marked improvement over the first in both team-spirit and actual scoring.

For this, our third year of endeavor, we are encouraged materially by the fact that tennis has been accepted and will be recognized by the Athletic Council as a Varsity enterprise, entitling one to the award of the Varsity "C" for a degree of proficiency in it.

Football

The 1937 football season presented the best record ever made by a Clarion team on the gridiron. The season ended with Clarion having won three and lost three. Much credit should be given Coach Tippin and his assistant for their work in building such a team composed largely of freshmen. However, a number of lettermen who returned provided a nucleus around which the team was built.

The team journeyed to Indiana for the opener with only two weeks to practice and lost 41-0. This one can be chalked up to inexperience.

The next week at Grove City the team made a much better showing and held the "Grovers" to a 7-6 win.

Alliance at home meant victory. The boys came through with 19-0 win.

Thiel at Greenville was somewhat a repetition of the Grove City game. Clarion lost 7-6.

Homecoming Day, Edinboro, brought sweet revenge. The team shoved Edinboro all over the field in the mud and emerged with a 6-0 victory.

The squad encountered California for the last tilt of the season, which proved to be the best game of the season. A kick blocked by Clarion early in the game netted the team two points which they jealously protected and threatened to increase several times before the final whistle. Clarion had beaten California for the first time in football history; only a 2-0 score, but still a victory.

SUMMARY OF SEASON

Indiana	41	Clarion—Away	0
Grove City	7	Clarion—Away	6
Alliance	0	Clarion—Home	19
Thiel	7	Clarion—Away	6
Edinboro	0	Clarion—Home	6
California	0	Clarion—Away	2
TOTAL	55		39

Manager

FRED MARSHALL—After the first two weeks of practice, Fred turned "Doc" at the request of the Coach. His duties for the rest of the year consisted of wrapping the boys up when the need occurred, and bringing them to when they passed out.

Trainer

LAWRENCE SMITH—"Smitty" was an efficient and proud manager. He not only managed the team in a business-like manner, but also gave the boys much encouragement.

Assistant Managers

Smitty's associates were Jim Imel and "Zit" Mooney. These positions, as well as those of trainer and manager, necessitate a great amount of work and entail great responsibility. The boys both rendered faithful service.

Football Lettermen

JOE ANDREO—Joe played his fourth year of football for the blue and gold and will be a hard man to replace. Alternated at tackle and fullback—particularly noted for his exceptional punting.

MIKE BEDZYK—This was Mike's fourth and last year of varsity football. Mike played under handicap of injuries but could always be depended on to give his best for the team—a triple threat man that will be hard to replace. Played quarterback this year.

HARRY WOZNIAK—A little guard that has what it takes. Wozzy always gave his best in every game and proved to be a hard man to get through. Finished his career on the gridiron this year.

EDDIE SCHIERBERL—Another senior that will be missed next year. Eddie is to be commended for his indominatable spirit and courage. A good tackle and great help to the team. Always there.

BUD KRIBBS—This was Bud's second year on the varsity squad and he proved to be a capable end—hard to get around and good on catching passes. Expect to hear more of him next year.

JIM MEYERS—Jim proved to be one of the best guards on the team by making the All-Northwestern Pennsylvania Team. Steady and dependable and a hard man to tackle. Second year on varsity squad.

MARSHALL TEETS—Marsh is another good end who could stretch out for passes at the right time. Second year on the team. Great things are expected of him in the future.

BILL SHERIDAN—A fast and illusive halfback; Bill should go places in his next three years at Clarion. Has indications of developing in a good triple-threat man.

HENRY PERSIGHETTI—Another freshman that made good. Henry or "Percy" is a hard, plunging fullback that is hard to stop. A good man on backing up the line.

Football Lettermen

BOB JEWELL—The fair-haired freshman tackle proved to be a little too tough for some of the boys. We look forward to seeing Bob in action next year.

WALT JOSEFCZYK—"Joe Alphabet" a freshman tackle was given the honor of being chosen for the All-American Unpronounceables. Joe has great possibilities.

RAY ABERCROMBIE—Ray plays best at a tackle position and proved himself very valuable in defense work, especially at California.

BILL LEE—A freshman end from Oil City who performed well in the latter part of the season. Intends to be back next year.

FELIX GALONSKI—Felix proved a good reserve guard who should work himself up into varsity material in the near future.

BILL BRATKOVICH—Bill is a steady, dependable center who saw action practically all the time. Has great possibilities.

WALT POLAND—A freshman reserve halfback. A tricky ball carrier, good passer, and nice blocker.

HOWARD WIDMANN—'Blinks' was a hard hitting guard who played good ball throughout the season. Alternated at center with Bratkovich.

CARL CHENEY—Alternated at halfback and fullback. Made excellent reserve material and should go places in the future.

HENRY BIRSA—Hank alternated on end with Bill Lee. Played exceptionally well on the defense. A hard man to get past.

"MULLET" WILLIAMS—Another freshman quarterback who proved himself varsity material. Called signals, was a good blocker, and excelled on defense.

Basketball

The 1937-38 basketball season was one of the most successful ever experienced by Clarion teams. The team won seven games and lost ten.

Coach Tippin whipped a capable squad together quickly, composed of four lettermen from last year, and the rest mainly freshmen.

Grove City defeated Clarion in the first game of the season 39-30.

As the first home game Penn State Extension was defeated 38-13.

After Christmas the squad journeyed to Edinboro and Alliance colleges, losing by close margins, 33-28 and 34-31 respectively.

The Indiana game here was another thriller, even though Clarion lost 38-42.

The California game here also was lost 42-35, and then Grove City took its second victory from Clarion 54-45.

Theil gave the team their second victory when the game ended 31-28 in favor of Clarion.

Slippery Rock brought another defeat, but Clarion, in her return game, held the green and whites to a six-point victory.

The heretofore unknown Mansfield team just wasn't strong enough, and Clarion emerged with a 32-26 win.

The California-Indiana trip netted the team two more defeats; 51-35 and 35-24 respectively.

Determined to make the season a good one the team entered the last lap looking like professionals and defeated Theil, 46-34; Edinboro 41-35; Penn State Extension 51-10; and Alliance 43-31.

Manager

FRED MARSHALL—'Pee Wee' served his second term as manager of the basketball squad. It is interesting to note that he was chosen for this position
twice during his college life—he must have been successful.

Assistant Manager

JOHN MOONEY—"Zit" too makes a habit of managing athletic teams. This year
he was assistant manager of both the football and the basketball teams. He
will in all probabilities become head manager next year.

Basketball Lettermen

MIKE BEDZYK—This was Mike's fourth and last year of college basketball. Mike has always been an integral part of the team—has lots of fight and that certain something that won't let him admit defeat. —Came out later because of injuries—best known as "Crip."

BRONIE SMOLAK—Another boy who has played his fourth and last year for Clarion—elected captain at the beginning of the season-"Smitak" or "Skinny" was a smooth, careful ball player and could always be depended on to steady the team.

BUD KRIBBS—Bud was the high scorer of the season and could always be depended on for four or five baskets a game—a hard cutting forward and a good man on defense—"Killer" is looking forward to one more year on the team.

JIM MEYERS—This was Jim's second year on the team. Known on the floor as "Monk" he is quiet but efficient—truly a stellar guard.

MARSHALL TEETS—Christened "Tapeworm," Marsh did a fine job in he forward position and under the basket on defense—second year on the team.

"STRETCH" CAMPBELL—Stretch came to us at the beginning of the second semester and was a welcome addition to the team—stepped into Abercrombie's shoes at center at Ray's departure from school.

HAROLD WILLIAMS—"Mullet" is another freshman on the squad that saw a great deal of action—did good work in the guard position.

JAMES IMEL—Jim's another freshman who saw much action at the forwad position—a good shot.

Autographs

FEATURE

Who's Who at Clarion

Clarion's Most and Best

MOST

likely to succeed
MORGAN JONES   MARIAN RENN
BILL MARSHALL   GERRY THORNE

typical student
BILL MARSHALL   PEGGY BOUQUIN
BUD KRIBBS   MARY JONES

wide awake in class
LAWRENCE SMITH   FERN BROOKS

wide awake out of class
PERRY LEWIS   AUDREY COYTE

BEST

sport
LAWRENCE SMITH   EVA MURDOCK
MIKE BEDZYK   EDITH DINSMORE

date
ED JACOBS   JUNE RHEA
PAUL GILTINAN   PAULINE HAY

dressed
BUD KRIBBS   FERN BROOKS
WALTER HASKELL   DOT STROUPE

line
CLAYTON VOGEL   EDITH DINSMORE
ROLAND KIRKLAND   ARDELLE WHITMAN

dancer
HAROLD BAILEY   RUTH EHMAN
BRONIE SMOLAK   FRANCES WHISNER

athlete
MIKE BEDZYK   GERRY THORNE
JIM MEYERS   EVA MURDOCK

prospective teacher
BRONIE SMOLAK   DORA BOARIO
LAWRENCE SMITH   GERRY THORNE

wit
PERRY LEWIS   GRACE GILES
HOMER HORNER   BETTY KANENGEISER

matched couple
MIKE BEDZYK   EVA MURDOCK
TOM PLYLER   JANE MAC MILLAN

loiterer
DON STROUPE   LOUISE HESS
CARL CHENEY   MARY JONES

movie of the year   *chapel program*
CONQUEST   GYROSCOPE
EMILE ZOLA   MASTER SINGERS

Ye Finale Examination

Name—Joe College.
Course—C. S. T. C.
Date—Sequelle Day.
Time—Eternity.

Multiple Choice Test

Example: Considered unnecessary for students of a teacher's college.

1. The Clarion Call is:
   a summons to the office, Jim, a publication.

2. Wilson's Woods is renowned as:
   a trysting place, a picnic ground, the habitat of ants.

3. Devereaux is:
   a French wine, a French premier, our personable new instructor.

4. Bud Wiser is:
   a beer, a freshman, a German city.

5. An eagerly anticipated event is:
   the college picnic, Sequelle Day, the end of the semester.

6. The "Clarion Call" is published:
   weekly, monthly, occasionally.

7. Student opinion favors construction of:
   a swimming pool, larger rose beds, non-slippery walks.

8. The library is a place to:
   make dates, sleep, be ejected from.

9. The day student men are noted for:
   breaking furniture, playing ping pong, making noise.

10. A's and B's are grades resulting from:
    apple shining, work, club participation.

11. Clarion's best swimming pool is:
    the lily pond, the basketball floor, a bathtub.

12. Anyone who remains over five minutes in class when the instructor is late is referred to as:
    an apple polisher, a diligent student, a foo.

13. Term papers are:
    copied, disliked, tardily submitted.

14. The quietest student on the campus is:
    Griffin, Lewis, Hummel.

15. These questions are:
    satiric, witty, foolish.

True-False Test

Place an F before the statement if it is true, a T if it is false.

1. C.S.T.C. is noted for its beautiful co-eds.
2. Teaching is the finest profession in the world.
3. C.S.T.C. increased its enrollment during the past years.
4. We expect an undefeated football team next fall.
5. Physics is a "snap" course.
6. "Foo" is a current slang term which means anything.
7. Student teachers delight in preparing lesson plans.
8. Mr Curll is proud of his nickname.
9. We always tell the truth when writing in someone's Sequelle.
10. This is the best Sequelle ever published.

Completion Test

1. The best fraternity is..............
2. The best sorority is..............
3. The..............is the local store most popular with college students.
4. Mr. Tippin's favorite expression is..............
5. Becht Hall food is..............
6. ....will be the next governor of Pennsylvania.
7. A friendship with..............is helpful in getting excused from class absences.
8. ....is a student whose name is difficult to spell.
9. ....was a chapel speaker who aroused much discussion.
10. ....is an instructor who gives difficult tests.

Do You Know Them?

College Humor

Central: Number please.

Lawrence Smith: Number; heck, I put a nickel in there and I want my chewing gum.

FABLE

Once upon a time, hundreds of years ago, there were four nice little girls, but that was once upon a time, hundreds of years ago.

Stroupe: Did you pass your exam, Win?

Port: Well, you see, it was like this—

Stroupe: Neither did I. Shake!

Miss Nair: There is someone in this room making a fool of himself. When he is through, I shall begin.

"I'm sorry. We've run out of gas."

"All right," was her instant reply, "I'll show you I'm game." And she had the tooth extracted without the gas.

Dr. Peirce (in class): Give me an example explaining the theory of like attracting like.

Shriver: I know a man who drank some wood alcohol and it went to his head.

The first year in college: "All that I am I owe to my mother."

The remaining years: All that I owe is paid by my father."

Jim Imel: I used to think you were dumb when I first met you.

Pauline Hay: Really?

Jim: But I wasn't sure of anything in those days.

Grace Giles: "What are you thinking about?"

Perry Lewis: "Thanks for the compliment."

When do the leaves begin to turn?

The night before the exams.

Mrs. Teets: This letter from Marshall is very short.

Mr. Teets: Yes, so is Marshall, or he wouldn't have written.

Morgan Jones: What would you do if someone were dying for a kiss?

Kay Snyder: Render first aid.

Basketball has its points, we agree. But the afternoon of a football game is the only time that you can walk down the street with a blonde on one arm and a blanket on the other without encountering raised eyebrows.

English Instructor: Are you smoking back there, Mr. Smith?

Smith: No, Sir, that's just the fog I'm in.

THE SEQUELLE STAFF THANKS THOSE PEOPLE THAT HELPED TO

MAKE THE ANNUAL A SUCCESSFUL BOOK

Modern Definitions

Monologue—a conversation between husband and wife.

Experience—What you know after making a fool of yourself.

Parasite—A person who goes through revolving doors on someone else's push.

Professor—A learned individual who can tell you who ruled Egypt in the fifth dynasty, but can't tell you where he left his umbrella.

Pajamas—A garment that is rolled up and put under the pillow to be used in case of fire.

Alibi—Trying to prove you were in class, where you weren't, in order to prove you weren't in the show, where you were.

Middle Ages—Any where between fifty and seventy.

Directions on School Books

1. One dose daily.

2. In case of fire throw this in.

3. Open at all hours?????

4. Shake well before using.

5. Handle with care.

6. A dose a day may keep C's and D's away.

7. Closed Saturdays and Sundays.

8. Apply both morning and night.

9. Open only in case of emergency.

10. Observe closely.

College Humor

CO-ED

She goes to college. She differs from her sister in that she is beautiful, for her features are delicate and regular, and her figure is a perfect 36. She uses cosmetics, but to accentuate her natural loveliness, and then only privately.

Her lips are red and kissable, but she does not use them to promiscuity. She is faithful to the owner of the fraternity pin she wears.

Her clothes are informal, in good taste. She carries them with an appealingly unconscious charm.

She studies hard, makes good grades. She does not employ soft-soap with her professors, nor does she cling about their necks.

She chews gum occasionally and smokes moderately. Her dancing is exquisite, but restrained.

Having no affectation, she does not attempt to employ a "line." Her great characteristic is her naturalness, her poise.

She does not exist.

TEN THINGS THE COLLEGE GIRL WILL NOT DO AFTER THE SHOW

1. Go to the morgue with you to identify stiffs.
2. Call up the Dean and ask him what time is it.
3. Help you window-shop for a new hat.
4. Discuss the chances on next year's World Series.
5. Help you see off your aunt at the depot.
6. Hitch-hike home—with you.
7. Quiz you on your calculus.
8. Give you a hair-cut.
9. Talk over your case of eczema.
10. Tell you what she uses to remove hair on arms and legs.

GO ON, READ IT

When you see
Something like this
Dragging all the way
Down the page
In a college annual,
Be assured,
It's only there
Because they have
Nothing funny,
Or clever,
Or smooth
To fill the space.

The bright young student look and thoughtfully at the second examination question, which read: "State the number of tons of coal shipped out of the United States in any given year."
Then his brow cleared and he wrote:
"1492—none."

Craftsmanship--

The finer material things of life are made by a fusion of the baser elements of nature with human aspiration---which finds expression in superior---CRAFTSMANSHIP

A high tribute to human intelligence is that man can take a piece of clay and make of it a thing of beauty. In all of the processes of this transformation there must be a guiding mind; that mind itself is guided by aspiration.

Skilled hands alone cannot produce the highest grade of printing. There must be aspiration to do better what thousands do well. There must be a combination of natural talent, knowledge gained from experience and, of course, the necessary tools.

Every printer has these in some degree. The difference between printers is the degree in which they have them. When they are present in a high degree, they result in beautiful and useful printing. The extent to which we have them, has gained for us a high appreciation among many patrons.

The Gray Printing Co.
DuBois and Falls Creek, Pennsylvania
Printers of the Nineteen Thirty-eight Sequelle

FROM THE PRESS OF
THE GRAY PRINTING COMPANY
DuBois, Pennsylvania

PLASTIC BINDING BY
STANDARD COLOR CARD & MFG. CO.
U. S. PAT. NO. 1,970,285, LIC. 16
BUFFALO, N. Y.

Lightning Source UK Ltd.
Milton Keynes UK
UKHW022115081218
333475UK00006B/191/P